D1213173

This edition published 1995 by Geddes & Grosset Ltd,
David Dale House, New Lanark, Scotland

Illustrated by Lyndsay Duff in the style of Charles Robinson

ISBN 1 85534 551 X

Printed in Slovenia

Little Bo-peep

Mother Goose Rhymes

Little Bo-peep

Little Bo-Peep

Little Bo-Peep has lost her sheep,
　And can 't tell where to find them;
Let them alone, and they 'll come home,
　And bring their tails behind them.

Little Bo-Peep fell fast asleep,
　And dreamt she heard them bleating;
And when she awoke, she found it a joke,
　For still they were all fleeting.

Then up she took her little
  crook,

Determined for to find them;

She found them indeed, but it made her heart bleed,
    For they 'd left all their tails behind them.

It happened one day as Bo-Peep did stray
    Into a meadow hard by,
There she espied their tails side by side,
    All hung on a tree to dry.

Little Bo-Peep

She heaved a sigh, and wiped her eye,
    And went over hill and dale, oh;
And tried what she could, as a shepherdess should,
    To tack to each sheep its tail, oh!

TO BED!

Come let's to bed,
Says Sleepy-head;
Sit up a while, says Slow;
Put on the pan,
Says Greedy Nan,
Let's sup before
we go.

OF GOING TO BED

Go to bed first,
　A golden purse;

Go to bed second,
A golden pheasant;

Go to bed third,
A golden bird.

THERE WAS A BUTCHER

There was a butcher cut his thumb,
When it did bleed, then blood did come.

There was a chandler making candle,
When he them stript, he did them handle.

There was a cobbler clouting shoon,
When they were mended, they were done.

There was a crow sat on a stone,
When he was gone, then there was none.

There was a horse going to the mill,
When he went on, he stood not still.

There was a lackey ran a race,
When he ran fast, he ran apace.

There was a monkey climbed a tree,
When he fell down, then down fell he.

There was a navy went into Spain,
When it return'd, it came again.

There was an old woman lived under a hill,
And if she's not gone, she lives there still.

WINTER·HAS·COME

Cold and raw
  the north
   wind doth blow,

    Bleak in a morning
      early;

All the hills are covered
    with snow,

    And winter 's now come
      fairly.

Monday's Child

M ONDAY'S child is fair of face,

Monday's Child

Tuesday's child is full
of grace,

Wednesday's child is full
of woe,

Thursday's child has far
to go,

Monday's Child

Friday's child is loving
and giving,

Saturday's child works hard
for its living,

But the child that is born
on the Sabbath day

Is bonny, and blithe, and
good, and gay.

I'LL TRY

Two Robin Redbreasts built their nest
  Within a hollow tree;
The hen sat quietly at home,
  The cock sang merrily;
And all the little ones said:
  "Wee, wee, wee, wee, wee, wee."

One day the sun was warm and bright,
  And shining in the sky,
Cock Robin said: "My little dears,
  'T is time you learned to fly;"
And all the little young ones said:
  "I'll try, I'll try, I'll try."

I know a child, and who she is
  I'll tell you by and by,
When Mamma says "Do this," or "that,"
  She says "What for?" and "Why?"
She'd be a better child by far
  If she would say "I'll try."

MASTER I HAVE

Master I have, and I am his man,
    Gallop a dreary dun;
Master I have, and I am his man,
And I'll get a wife as fast as I can;
With a heighty gaily gamberally,
    Higgledy, piggledy, niggledy, niggledy,
      Gallop a dreary dun.

ROCK-A-BY, BABY

ROCK-A-BY, baby, thy cradle is green;
    Father's a nobleman, mother's a
      queen;
    And Betty's a lady, and wears a
      gold ring;
    And Johnny's a drummer, and
      drums for the king.

THERE WAS A MAN

THERE was a man, and he had naught,
  And robbers came to rob him;
He crept up to the chimney pot,
  And then they thought they had
    him.

But he got down on t' other side,
  And then they could not find him;
He ran fourteen miles in fifteen days,
  And never looked behind him.

JACK'S FIDDLE

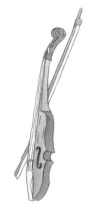

Jacky, come give me thy fiddle,
  If ever thou mean to thrive.
Nay, I 'll not give my fiddle
  To any man alive.

If I should give my fiddle
  They 'll think that I 'm gone mad;
For many a joyful day
  My fiddle and I have had.

A
was an
archer

was an Archer, and shot at a Frog

was a Butcher, and kept a Bull-dog

was a Captain, all covered with Lace

was a Drunkard, and had a Red Face

E e

was an Esquire, with insolent Brow

F f

was a Farmer, and followed the Plough

G g

was a Gamester, who had but Ill Luck

H h

was a Hunter, and hunted a Buck

I i

was an Innkeeper, who loved to Bouse

was a Joiner, and built up a House

was King William, once governed this Land

was a Lady, who had a White Hand

was a Miser, and hoarded up Gold

was a Nobleman, Gallant and Bold

was an Oyster Wench, and went about Town

was a Parson, and wore a Black Gown

was a Queen, who was fond of good Flip

was a Robber, and wanted a Whip

was a Sailor, and spent all he got

was a Tinker, and mended a Pot

was a Usurer, a miserable Elf

was a Vintner, who drank all Himself

was a Watchman, and guarded the Door

was Expensive, and so became Poor

was a Youth, that did not love School

was a Zany, a silly old Fool

A was an apple pie

B bit it,

C cut it,

D dealt it,

E eat it,

F fought for it,

G got it,

H had it,

J joined it,

K kept it,

L longed for it,

M mourned for it,